Little to Spare & Nothing to Waste
A Brighton Boyhood in the Hungry Thirties

by Robert Haywaɪ

CONTENTS

Opposite: Sun Street, a few yards behind Grand Parade

Brighton Books Publishing

11 Sussex Street, the author's home, note the barber's pole

Introduction

11 Sussex Street, where I was born in 1918, consisted of six rooms, all small and low-pitched: a living room with an open fireplace or grate on which most of the cooking was done, a front room which housed the barber's shop, three bedrooms, the windows of two overlooking Sussex Street, and a back bedroom where the window looked down on a small backyard. The stone-floored scullery contained a gas cooker overlit by a gas-lamp, and a copper, where the washing was done, it being the pleasant duty of one of the boys to keep the fire underneath well fuelled when the weekly wash was in progress, with cardboard boxes obtained from the nearby sweet shop.

The primitive privy, where once a rat was spied, and with no shortage of spiders, was in a dark corner at the rear of the scullery. When a younger, more nervous member of the family wished to visit after dark, they were invariably accompanied by an older sibling, who stood by and rather shakily held the candle.

The coal-hole was in the living room, under the staircase behind a door. There was always a cat, to keep the mice at bay. On the hob of the open fire stood a great, soot-blackened cast-iron pot, at times with narrow-bones and lentils, or a bacon or a suet pudding slowly cooking.

Foreword

I have, endeavoured to depict the activities and pastimes of a schoolboy during the lean years of the nineteen-thirties, and to capture the atmosphere of the time in one of Brighton's poorest quarters. The 'thirties were a different age, life passed at a slower pace than today, not all greed and speed, tastes were simpler, standards of morality and behaviour were higher. The sons - and their sons - of the men born and bred in these districts, live in a different, more affluent world, running cars and often owning their own houses and businesses. The youngsters of the time had a happy childhood, despite the privations. Money never worried or troubled them, they saw so little of it. If they were fortunate enough to possess a penny they were rich indeed.

Many of the day-to-day events had an earthy flavour, often spiced with a touch of ribald humour. The 'thirties were also times of great change and social reforms. Bleak years of economic depression, unemployment, penny-pinching, when a little money had to go a long way with much foraging and great culinary ingenuity to feed large families. These were the days when 'Uncle', the pawnbroker, ran a profitable business; the 'tally-man' made his rounds, calling from door to door. These were also the days when the landlord would call personally for his rent.

A motor-car was a rare sight in the area, many of the thoroughfares were in any case too narrow, so the children played their organised games in safety. The car was slowly ousting the horse, and steam-power was at its zenith, soon to decline. These changing times, these pre-war years - the troubled calm before the storm - witnessed the hey-day of the cinema, 'the pictures' as they were called.

Boys were full of mischief and pranks, the local youth of the time being no exception, but in the different values of the 'thirties there was no vandalism and no hooliganism. So, many of the once-familiar things are gone. Those who knew them will no doubt welcome their remembrance, those that did not may like to know a little of how the poor lived.

In these recollections some ornamentation has been made here and there. No doubt there are also errors and omissions. Throughout this task I have met only help and encouragement. I thank those who have given information and loaned prints and pictures, with particular mention of a niece, Mrs. Glennis Tricker, for typing the manuscript, and of a brother David, for revising and correcting it, and offering advice and assistance; and Marie Mansbridge for typesetting the text.

Robert R. Hayward

They Called Them Slums

Much of Brighton's architecture remains; the magnificent crescents, squares and terraces have been preserved. The old working-class districts that once housed many of those in service with the well-to-do in the large houses, built at approximately the same time, have long-since been demolished. They were part of the town's history, but only the memories remain.

Sussex Street was tucked away behind the tall facade of Grand Parade and hemmed-in at the top of the hill by the Tarner Estate and allotments - known to the locals as the Back Hill, a warren of narrow streets, rows, courts, alleys, twittens and cul-de-sacs. Having been built during the days of horse-traffic there were also mews and stables. Constructed piecemeal over the years in a happy-go-lucky fashion, without benefit - or blight - of town-planning. Building styles were varied, though many of the houses were built of fist-sized beach boulders set in mortar.

Some streets were of uniform design, in others the line of the roof-tops rose and fell raggedly as if a house had been shoved in a gap here and there. In Sussex Street there was one such as this, a tall, narrow dwelling, one room wide up all its storeys, known as The Rabbit Hutch.

A little way up the hill was Ivory Buildings - a cul-de-sac - also called The Bricks, as its road surface was paved with thin red bricks set on edge, as if tiled. One side of The Bricks was houses, the other, on a higher level, was the playground of Richmond Street School. When the kids were at play here, a mother could lean out of a bedroom window and very nearly hand her children their lunch, so narrow was the alley in between. In these cul-de-sacs and canyonned courts, the lower rooms were dark and the outlook dismal, the only view a blank wall, a yard or two away, on the hottest of days, these sunless alleys were damply cool. Some backyards were mere crevasses between houses, whereas other residents were fortunate in possessing a small back garden or backyard. Here a few fowls were kept, some being breeds never seen today, such as: Buff Orpington, White Wyandotte, White and Black Leghorns, Dorkings, Faverolles and Minorcas. The business of poultry-keeping gave rise to another - gritting.

The iron-shod cart-wheels grinding over the stony ways produced plenty of shards, splinters, and flinty grit, which was swept up and sold by the bucketful to the grateful chicken owners. Another way to earn an honest penny was by 'dunging', searching the streets and mews with a barrow and shovel for horses 'doughnuts'; highly-valued by allotment-holders.

Rabbit-hutches took up little space in the back-yards and were cheaply and easily constructed. The breeding and fattening of these passive and prolific animals was a profitable venture, usually the hobby of the youngsters in the family. Levetts, the corn chandlers, in Gloucester Road sold hay and straw for the rabbits, and food for poultry. It was an interesting place, with a rural air about it. Along the wall stood a row of large wooden bins, holding the various grains, with a large shiny scoop. One could not pass Levetts without sneaking in and thrusting both hands deep into the bins letting the grain trickle through the fingers. Hay was stored on an upper floor, compact bales cut from the stack with the great wide-bladed, double-handled knife, hauled up by gantry from the farm-wagon below. The arrival of a load of hay was a welcome event and was soon noised abroad; the loose strands that fell from the bales were eagerly gleaned from the road and pavement by the rabbit-keepers.

Children in the Carlton Hill area in the 1930s

Accessible by way of a mews or twitten, there were a number of yards or courtyards - quiet, secluded spaces or squares. Such was Elliot's, or White's Yard, at the end of Sussex Mews, the first turning on the left up Sussex Street from Grand Parade. Here you were away from it all and in farm-like surroundings, and stamping in the stables would be a horse or two. In the hay-loft the sun-dried grass and shrivelled meadow flowers scented the warm and dusty air; in the yard Chanticleer strutted among his harem of hens as they pecked and scratched among the cobbles, only the cows were missing. From this tranquil pastoral retreat, where at first light the crowing of the cock awoke the sleeping neighbourhood, it was but a stone's throw to where the main London to Brighton Road ran noisily and busily past. Over the roof-tops, in Grand Parade, was a different world.

Our district of the town, embracing Richmond Street, Sussex Street and Carlton Hill, with many small houses tightly set in the close lying streets, was said to be one of the most densely populated areas in England, it teemed with children. Into these districts, fleeing from poverty and politics - came the Italians, a frugal, hard-working, peaceable people, they fell among friends. In the dog-days of summer an Italian atmosphere pervaded the neighbourhood. Not far away, on the borders of Edward Street, their Romany ways forsaken, but in a perpetual state of hostility with their neighbours, dwelt the gipsies. Another familiar sight was the fishermen coming home from the sea, in tan frocks and leather thigh-boots, carrying a bucket of fish in the crook of the arm.

There was squalor here and there in the neighbourhood, as there is sometimes now, with higher living standards and better housing conditions. By and large, despite the penny-pinching times, a general standard of decency and cleanliness was maintained, many of the humble homes were kept like palaces. In the cosy kitchen the polished kettle sang on the black-leaded hob, sprawled in front of the glowing range the fat cat purred and on the dressers and sideboards, the bric-a-brac and brassware sparkled like the stars. Hanging by many a door would be the brass or pewter milk jug, which the milkman on his round would fill - generally with skimmed milk - from the churn. A number of households kept a song-bird, a linnet or skylark, on fine days the cage would be hung over the door or on the wall of the house.

Compared with modern conditions, life was primitive. On washing days the fire was lit under the copper in the scullery - often a dungeon of a place, brick-floor, small-window and poorly ventilated. In the sauna-like atmosphere, by the wan light of the flickering flame of the gas-jet, the steaming, soda-steeped clothes would be raked from the boiling cauldron and soaped and scrubbed on the wooden wash-board. A week or two before Christmas, the Christmas pudding would be cooked in the same copper.

It was remarkable how some of these small dwellings housed such large families. Somewhere in the crowded menage it was not unusual to find a widowed grandmother, an integral part of the household, she would bring up the youngsters - raise a second brood, while the mother went out 'charring' or some such menial task, to earn a few bob. Although kids thought the world of their gran, with her funny old-fashioned ways, they were not beyond saucing her and playing up sometimes. Should the mother of a young family meet a premature death, gran would step in and run the bereaved household.

Within the confines of this old-established locality there dwelt a tightly-knit community, neighbourly people, largely living amicably, ever-ready with sympathy and help if trouble came. In this village-like atmosphere, everybody knew one another - and most of each other's business! You could not be distant or aloof if you wanted to, you lived too near your neighbours. A close company, bound together by the toils of hardship, hard living and hard work, sharing life's ups and downs. Resilient, resourceful people; rearing their large families in a law-abiding and god-fearing manner who, in spite of bleak economic conditions, managed by dint of frugality, hard work and sacrifice, to keep them cleanly-clothed and well fed. The children represented the wealth of the community and brought families closer together. You had your pals and would visit their homes and be welcome, and they in yours.

The seller of water-cress cum clandestine bookmaker, the maker and purveyor of hokey-pokey, the sweep, the tinsmith, the cobbler, the baker, the barber, the butcher, the grocer, the publican, the wreath-maker, were all your neighbours. It was - to a large extent - a self-contained community.

A number of youngsters of school age had a Saturday job, the most popular and sought-after being those connected with the food trades, such as the butcher and baker. After helping the baker on his rounds - by means of horse and cart - his keen young assistant got one-and-sixpence for the day's work and a bonus of a bag of stale cakes or a loaf or two. The butcher would supplement his pay with a pig's head or some such delicacy. Hoskins, the coal merchant rewarded his boy for his 5½ day week with the princely sum of five shillings, plus 7lb bag of coal.

The gin-palaces had long since gone, to be replaced by the beer-shops; one of the major causes of the hardship and poverty. Even the pub names change with the times, gone are The Yacht, The Yacht Anchor, The Flyman's Home, The Highbury Barn, The Sack of Shavings, and so on. At one time in Edward Street there were said to be 39 pubs, one on practically every corner: the Turners, the Plasterers, the Painters and the Italian Arms. Supplying the numerous pubs were the local breweries, many being small family concerns, including: Tamplins, Smithers, Rock, Cannon, Kemp Town, Kidd and Hotblacks.

The annual outing of the Royal Yacht public house in Sussex Street

Most of the pubs held an Annual Outing or Beano - or booze-up - for their customers. On the morning of the great day, the solid-tyred char-a-banc stood outside the pub and the beer was stowed aboard. Adding to the fun the publican would appear with a shovelful of nearly red-hot pennies, and scatter them in the road. The kids, would hop and skip about as they tried to pick up the hot coins, throwing them from hand to hand, scorching their fingers, and spinning them in the air to cool. The Beano would leave to the cheers of the crowd. In the evening, the sound of beery singing coming from afar heralded their homecoming, and neighbours gathered to welcome them back.

Despite the fact that the houses - indeed the entire locality - was condemned as being unfit for human habitation, and was ultimately demolished, the standard of health was reasonably high. In these old districts of the town, sanitation left much to be desired, drainage was poor and rats were sometimes seen. Mice abounded, so every household kept a cat, bed-bugs were a curse. The old houses, constructed of lath and plaster and woodwork, warped and cracked with the years, provided plenty of lurking places for these foul insects, making their control difficult. Where an infestation occurred, fumigation was the most satisfactory method of dealing with them, the chimney was bunged-up with a sack, the windows and doors sealed, and a sulphur candle left burning in the room, to drive them through the crumbly walls and draughty lofts into the next-door neighbour's bedrooms.

Tuberculosis, or consumption, was probably the cause of many deaths. Diphtheria, that cruel killer of the young, was said to emanate from foul drains. Scarlet Fever was another highly infectious disease, meriting isolation in the 'Sanny' off Bear Road. Another disease that affected children was rickets, brought about by malnutrition. The National Health Service had yet to be born, so the doctor charged a fee when called to the home of a patient. He was usually called only when the situation was serious - lest it should prove to be a false alarm. These devoted doctors, never pressed too hard for a long-owed fee.

In the event of the death of a child of the neighbourhood - if not from a contagious disease - the friends of the deceased would be allowed to pay their last respects and view the corpse lying in the coffin on the table in the darkened front room. The little group of silent youngsters, would stand and sheepishly stare, too young to comprehend the dreadful finality of Death.

Keeping law and order in the locality were the constables Tricky Albert and Forty-guts, ever-ready to administer summary justice on the spot. It was advisable to give these two lawmen a wide berth, as they were greatly given to flicking your ears with their gloves when passing, to encourage good behaviour in the future. During the decade 1925-1935, many went to bed at night never troubling to bolt their front doors, children were often sent on night errands to the shops, open until late in the evening, particularly the chemists. Despite the dark and often deserted streets, they did so without fear.

Life's Tapestry

Apart from their own games and pastimes, the carefree days of the young were enlivened by the bustle of life that went on around them. Itinerant hawkers would go about their lawful - or unlawful - business shouting their wares, travelling tradesmen would solicit work from door to door and ply their craft at the kerbside.

The Water Cart

Many of the streets and roads were unmade, flinty and rough. In the hot, dry weather the dust would blow about and the pavements became gritty underfoot. Then the horse-drawn water-cart, a large metal tank on wheels, connected to a tube at the rear, finely perforated to produce a spray would come around. When in operation on a Summer's day, a band of boys and girls would follow close behind, enjoying the cooling jets on their bare legs and feet.

The Pitch-Boiler

A horse-drawn pitch-boiler came to surface some of the stonier streets and to renew the worn coating of the made-up roads; an object of great interest to all small boys. A fire burned under the great round barrel boiler, to keep the black and sticky substance flowing smoothly. Attached to the boiler was a long-handled pump which forced the hot pitch down a flexible tube and out of the nozzled spray at the end. The horse, led slowly with many stops and starts, whilst at the rear, wielding the hissing spray in rhythmic sweeps over the road-surface, walked a tar-baby. Like a knight in shiny black armour, he was protected from chin to ankles by a thick apron; on his feet were heavy clogs, all covered in pitch. His hot and smoky occupation encouraged a fondness for drink. The strong coal-tar fumes from the pitch-boiler were reputed to have healing properties for respiratory ailments and particularly helpful in cases of whooping-cough. It was common to see sufferers, including mothers with sickly youngsters in their arms, standing to leeward of the pitch-boiler inhaling the effusions.

The Ice Man

In the warm weather, the ice-man came to deliver to the local fishmongers, butchers and ice cream vendors, these being pre-refrigerator days. The glistening ice was stowed in eighteen-inch cubes aboard a primitive open lorry, and were handled with a large pair of sharply-pointed tongs. As some of his customers only required half a cube, the ice-man would chip a deep groove in the middle of all four sides by deft use of an ice-pick; then he would drive a wide chisel into the groove and the block would fall neatly in half. Meanwhile, his youthful audience would be darting about retrieving the flying ice-chips and popping them in their mouths as a free substitute for ice-cream. On one particular hot day the ice man attempted to take his lorry up Sussex Street. He got about half-way up the steep incline when his cargo shifted and the heavy ice-cubes slid backwards like an avalanche, burst through the wooden tail-board, hitting the ground in a shower of ice-splinters. When they had slithered to the bottom of the hill, they were surrounded by a horde of youngsters, who fell on their knees and licked the ice chippings.

The Dairyman

Milk was delivered to the door and many householders hung a pint or half-pint pewter pots or jugs by the door, which the milkman filled up, or they brought their jugs to the churn on the cart. The day's milk came in a churn by rail to the station. At the top of Trafalgar Street he would grasp the boss in the centre of the lid with one hand, tilt the churn on to the edge of its bottom rim and start her rolling. The clatter of his hob-nailed boots as he ran down the hill, coupled with the bell-like clanging of the revolving lid, gave forewarning of his approach and cleared his way.

The Knife Grinder

An interesting visitor, who never lacked an audience, was the knife and scissors grinder. Going from door to door, he would collect the blunted instruments, returning to his workshop on wheels. There were variants of this simple machine, but, the works were always set between a pair of tall, spidery wheels. The handles protruded well out aft and were bolted to a pair of strong uprights that acted as legs when the grindery was stationary. Set low were two boards acting as pedals, a long metal rod attached to the end of each of these was cranked to and turned a large wheel set centrally, this carried a belt that drove the grindstone. As a refinement, some models had a can of water suspended over the stone, in the bottom of the can a very fine hole was bored to allow the water to drip slowly onto the spinning stone.

When operating, the knife-grinder sat on a board placed across the handles and pedalled away as if playing a harmonium. As he pedalled, he applied the steel to the stone with a harsh hiss, and the sparks flew merrily.

"Chairs to Mend?"

Another travelling tradesman was the chair-mender. "Chairs to mend?", he would cry in the street. Sitting on a stool in a quiet corner, he would practise his craft. Squatting on the pavement around him, the kids admired and envied him as his nimble fingers weaved, twisted and plaited the rushes and split cane.

Barrow Business

Street cries, once a common sound, are heard no more, one of the last being that of the rag-and-bone man. In a society that had little to spare and nothing to waste, what would be rubbish today was saved, with an eye to its future disposal for a little profit. So the rag-and-bone man would also take jam-jars, bottles and rabbit-skins. These being very much the kids' perks, the artful rag-and-bone man would offer goldfish in lieu of money.

One or two local residents followed the time-honoured calling of 'totting', these free-ranging, shrewd bargainers scoured the better-class neighbourhoods for 'tots' - mostly second hand clothing. On their return home, they would sort out the day's haul on the pavement, where, if any neighbours looking on saw something that took their fancy, they stood the chance of picking it up cheaply. Two particular totters come to mind, Bugling Totter, who announced his presence by sending forth shrill blasts on a battered bugle, and Ginger Totter.

Akin to the totters was 'Bed-tick Annie', who specialised in buying, repairing and selling mattresses, bolsters, pillows, and particularly bed-ticks, and who doubtless came across plenty of livestock during the course of her transactions.

These street-traders used a hand-barrow for their business. If they did not own one, they could be hired from the local black-smiths by the day, for a small charge. A large number of home removals were carried out by hand-barrow, particularly the moonlight flit. When families were behind with the rent, they would up-sticks in the night, first making sure that the house they were moving into was not owned by the same landlord as the one they had just vacated.

Chimney Sweep

The Lamplighter

In all weathers, as dusk fell, the lamplighter came on his rounds and lit-up the darkening streets. He rode a bicycle and, without stopping or dismounting, as he came to each gas-lamp he would reach up with his long pole and deftly pull down the lever, setting off the mellow light; then turning them off again in the morning. His night's sleep varied with the seasons - long in the winter, short in the summer.

Coal to Woburn

Mr. Hoskins, the local coal-merchant, had his business at the corner of Woburn Place and Sussex Street. Access was difficult for a heavily-laden vehicle, as it necessitated a sharp right-hand turn into a narrow street from the steep hill. The long, horse-drawn cart, loaded with coal and coke, would turn into Sussex Street from Grand Parade and come to a halt a short distance from the bottom of the hill, where a pair of trace-horses would be harnessed at the front, making a team of four. While these preparations were taking place, a large crowd of kids would be gathering in anticipation. The carter would crack his whip and shout, the horses would lunge forward, all the slack gear would tighten up with a snap and a jerk, and off they would go in a wild charge up the sharp gradient. The carter clumped along in his hob-nailed boots at the head of the lead-horse, followed by an excited horde of cheering youngsters running alongside. Up the hill, slowing as the slope steepened, the kids urging the horses on with their shouts, the shaggy hooves slipped and clattered, the sparks darted as the steel shoes struck the flinty road, as they pulled the creaking cart up and around the corner into the flat side street.

Tales by Firelight

The night-watchman on road-works and construction sites, would take over and stand guard throughout the night when the navvies and builders had finished their day's work, tending the oil-lamps and stoking the fire. Elderly men or those with a war disability often did this lonely job, so most of them welcomed a little young company. A few boys would be allowed to sit in his snug and warm hut, while the wintry wind drummed against the canvas walls.

How The Poor Lived

These were the 'Hungry 'Thirties'; bleak times of economic depression, unemployment was rife and money tight but nobody starved, though many fasted. Many families still had recourse to the soup kitchen, but to others this smacked of charity, and they were only driven there when in most desperate straits. Long days of hard work by parents pulled the large families through the bad times. The author's mother supplemented the family's precarious income by dressmaking for the neighbours. When the youngsters were tucked in bed, and the house was quiet, out would come the sewing machine, and to the soft hiss and in the pale light of the gas mantle, work would sometimes go on until 2 am in order to finish a job and bring in a little money.

Many of the breadwinners in the neighbourhood were self-employed men, whose income was precarious and whose fortunes fluctuated, but day after day, something appetising appeared on the table, nothing was wasted. By dint of keen foraging, and the knowledge of where cheap raw material could be obtained, a little money was made to go a long way and you ate the plain food placed before you.

The storing and handling of food left much to be desired, if the mice made merry with the cheese while the cat slept on the sack of sugar, and the flies feasted on the fish-paste, it was all part of the living conditions of the time.

Cunning psychology was often employed by the cook when funds were low and a particularly mean and unpopular dinner was served, such as cow's udder. Somehow one became convinced that one was eating roast beef, whilst lip-sticking pork-rind soup could, be made to taste like mock-turtle. The bony bits of meat and offal were cheap and used as the basis of a simple and filling dinner. A twopenny marrow-bone, boiled, with the addition of lentils made a good soup, or the marrow could be tapped out when sufficiently cooked, and spread on bread, like butter. Sixpennyworth of bullock's cheek - now called ox cheek and sold as pet food - with pot-herbs (onions, swedes, turnips, etc.) costing a penny or two, made a savoury stew. A sheep's head could be bought for sixpence.

The brains in a 6d sheep's head were a great delicacy, half a pig's head made a tasty brawn; 'Scotch pianos' (breasts of lamb), dish of 'block ornaments' (mixed meat pieces and trimmings) was highly appreciated, particularly when curried. Chitterlings (or 'chidlings') - being part of the small intestine of the humble and prolific pig - were an acquired taste. When despatched to buy a sheep's head, one was sometimes instructed to light-heartedly tell the butcher to cut it as near the arse as possible, or on another occasion to ask for 'sixpenn'orth of chiddlings, and no hodge (dung)'.

A giblet pie was a great treat, with giblets bought at Hudson's in East Street. Buyers would sit in a row on the low wall in front of the Town Hall, passing the time spent waiting by singing or fighting. Every now and again, an employee of Hudson's would step out on to the pavement holding a parcel of giblets aloft, and call a boy's name. The chosen one would dash forward, tender his sixpence, and be handed his purchase. Only certain boys were called, you could sit there all day and get nothing.

Opposite: rear of Albion Street

One took a basin to Boltons in Gardner Street for twopennyworth of cracked eggs, and go to Mence Smith in North Road for black treacle. Still in the unrefined condition in which it left the West Indies, the molasses was stored in a battered barrel, chocked-up on wooden trestles and fitted with a wooden tap. As the viscous treacle ran forth in a thin black stream, the shopman had no time to waste, so a child was left to hold a jam-jar under the tap.

Bread and dripping was popular, mainly for high tea, particularly the brown jelly at the base. Dripping was quickly snapped up when on sale, a speciality with a butcher-cum-cooked-meat shop in Richmond Street. When a fresh consignment appeared in the window up would go the cry in the street: 'Dripping at Eggars!', and a dash indoors for a basin and money, with a rush to the shop. Pork crackling was pared off the roasted joint and sold separately and cheaply.

Puddings, solid and sustaining, were the belly-fillers. Plum duff, spotted dick, or spotted dog, date pudding, bread pudding, etc., and a great favourite - bacon pudding. To cater for a variety of family tastes, and requiring only one cooking, a triple specimen with bacon and onions at one end, bacon only at the other, and a sort of gastronomic no-man's-land of plain pudding in the middle, to be garnished with jam or treacle.

Serving the town were a large number of small bakeries, mostly family concerns, delivering by horse-and-cart or by barrow and basket. Among them were Prices, Nappers, Mephams, Hollinghams, Goldsmith and Towner, Cuttress and many more. Stale-bread could be purchased for a few pence and carried home in a pillow-case. The hardest loaves would be soaked, fruit added and turned into a bread pudding.

In the grocer's shops of the 'thirties practically everything was sold loose and in the smallest quantities - a pennyworth of tea, sugar, marg, etc. You could take your dish for jam, or if you fancied welsh rarebit for tea, purchase a handful or two of cheese-rinds. Most commodities came in bulk from the wholesalers, including salmon, shrimp, and meat paste, large pink cubes stood in the window or on the counter, the right amount being cut out for each customer. Tea was sold direct from the plywood tea-chest, so if the time was ripe, you could ask for ha'p'orth of dust tea, the residue at the bottom of the chest, which you were left to extract yourself, pinching some of the tin-foil at the same time.

The muffin man came around, toting his wares in a large tray deftly balanced on his head and ringing a bell to warn of his approach. Another travelling tradesman with a good head for business, was the trotter man. He would reach up and select a boiled pig's foot, spread a daub of mustard on it, slap the tasty trotter into a sheet of newspaper, take your money give change, blow his nose with one finger, and proceed on his way, all without taking the tray from his head.

There could be faggots and pease pudding for supper, or perhaps fish and chips - a penny huss-flap and ha'p'orth of chips. The dross and skimmings of the seething fryer, known as 'scraps', were often free. Fish was plentiful and cheap. These were the days when the great herring and mackerel shoals ran through the Channel, when in one night's fishing, a haul of over 250 stone of herring was not unusual.

Skate pie, huss pie, or a hybrid pie of skate and huss; kibling (small skate); spatters (small plaice); slips (small sole); the kittlemaw (monk fish), repulsive to the eye, but delightful to the taste, being sold as scampi; pin-dogs (small huss); cod's heads, about a third of the weight of the entire fish, carrying a lot of flesh and ideal for fish-cakes, the eyes being a trifle gristly; all graced the tables of the poor. Mackerel in the summer, herring in the winter, the latter, so rich and full of goodness, were hawked through the neighbourhood and sold as cheaply as 16 or more for a shilling at times of glut. Had you walked through these now-vanished streets early on a December evening, from practically every house there issued the smell of fish cooking, it seemed the entire community was sitting down to a tea of fried herrings.

As the weekly wage was received on Friday afternoon or Saturday morning, the week-end shopping took place on Saturday evening, when most shops remained open until late, the time when the butchers auctioned their meat. This was a jolly highlight of the week for many, with the boisterous crowd gathered in front of the open shop-front, making bid and counter-bid, the proceedings being further enlivened by much banter, with many a great aitch-bone knocked down to about 18 pence, and carried off in triumph. Some Brighton butchers had names appropriate to their trade: Bullock, Leaney, Pidgeon. Before being moved to its present site, the Open Market occupied the pathway that bisects the Level, and late on Saturday evening presented an animated scene, with the bustling throng, and stalls lit by the hissing naphtha flares.

Dogbellies and Babies' Heads

If one wished to eat out, there was an eating-house at the bottom of Carlton Hill. The bill of fare never varied greatly and the tempting window display would have delighted a gourmet. In the centre lay a baron of beef (or horse), garnished with a halo of bluebottles; to the left lay a paving-slab of bread-pudding; on the right stood a basin of dripping; eaten by the down-at-heel dwellers of the nearby doss-houses. At Barbers restaurant you could purchase long meat puddings known as dogbellies, or round ones known as babies' heads.

Devilled Jackavells and Limpet Chowder

During the appropriate season, an expedition would be despatched to Black Rock for a dish of winkles, or, for the epicure, a bowl of broiled limpets. The common shore crabs - known in the vernacular as 'Jackavells' - were captured for the pot.

'Dead 'Uns'

The flower-seller and wreath-maker, was a well-known and picturesque figure in her long black skirt, black button-up boots, white blouse and white apron, stiff with starch. Her pitch was for many years outside Hanningtons in North Street, and by virtue of this she had contacts for cheap grub with some of the traders in the vicinity. One of these was The Creamery in Pavilion Buildings, and it was always a sweet chore to accompany one of her boys to collect the stale cakes ('dead 'uns'), for on the way home one was often rewarded with a chocolate eclair or some such rare treat.

Slum Saturday

The majority of those fortunate to be in employment, worked a 5½-day week, finishing around mid-day on Saturday. The wages taken home - some minus the pub score - with prospect of the week-end leisure ahead, produced a holiday spirit in the neighbourhood. This was encouraged by the variety of musical entertainment regularly provided in the streets on a Saturday: the well-known counter-tenor, Tommy Sinden, entertained the queues waiting outside the Theatre Royal and the Court Cinema. Here he would tumble about in the road, stand on his head, play the bones and the mouth organ, and render music-hall ditties in a thin tremolo.

As none of the houses in the area had a bathroom the locals visited North Road Slipper Baths on a Saturday to remove the week's grime.

I remember a few regular events of a Saturday, such as:

Beer-Barrel Polka
Barrel-organs would go the round of the public houses, a peg-legged man living in the area employed a donkey to pull his instrument. After singing a chorus or two, the regulars within, merry with a skinful of stout, and infected by the jog-trot rhythm of the jangling melodies, would, hitch up their skirts, and nimbly execute the Kidd and Hotblack jig. The peg-legged man was said to stable his donkey in his front room.

Bella Musica
Every Saturday dinner-time, the wizened Neapolitan with his hurdy-gurdy mounted on a pram chassis would arrive and station himself in Grand Parade, close to the bottom of Sussex Street. Grinding away at the handle, he would regale the cognoscenti with the bella musica of his homeland, setting them whistling and humming the old songs of Italy.

The Coronation
For many, a visit to the 'pictures' made a welcome break at the week-end, although it often meant queuing for admission on a Saturday evening or a rainy Sunday afternoon. In the morning, if funds permitted, the younger set, for the princely sum of 3d., would receive their weekly ration of culture at the Coronation Cinema, near the bottom of North Road. The balcony was miniscule, whilst the seats in the darker pit were individual and upholstered, and much favoured, at times other than Saturday mornings, by the local young bloods and their doxies. The stalls were long, wooden forms, and into these the boys and girls were packed tight. Some of the youngsters brought bottles of transparent lemonade, and turned the occasion into a sort of picnic. Before the performance, the lady pianist would walk down the aisle to her instrument, the manager, would then get the kids to sing the current hit-tune 'Ain't she sweet?'.

Harold Lloyd, Buster Keaton, etc, caused the laughter, whilst the rapid gun-fire of unerring accuracy of such masters of the lightning draw as Tom Mix, Buck Jones, Tim McCoy and the like provided the thrills. These were silent films, but the youthful patrons of the art waxed vociferous at moments of tension in the screenplay, advising the hero to "Look behind yer!" or to "Shoot!", when his position became desperate.

The projection apparatus was primitive, the film would occasionally break, causing a delay while repairs were carried out. If this hiatus proved lengthy, the manager would mount the stage and lead the audience in a sing-song, lest they became restive. During a short interval midway through the programme, when there would be a concerted rush to the privy, or when the lemonade would be swigged and the bottle passed on, the major-domo sweetened the air of the auditorium with a disinfectant spray. The emergency exit was by way of a short out-door passage, the door at the end opening into Cheltenham Place, and the gents' lavatory. Crafty boys, by prior arrangement, on the excuse of answering the call of nature, would sneak from their seats and surreptitiously slip the inner bolt of the exit door, thus enabling their mates to 'bunk in at the back'. On the way home after the morning matinee, scenes from the cowboy film would be re-enacted in the Victoria Gardens, until the arrival of a copper.

Signor S.
The industrious Italians' main occupations were making and selling hokey-pokey in the summer and roasting and selling hot chestnuts in the winter evenings. When the days began to shorten, the flowery barrow would be stripped of its trappings and the Italian flag; then fire would replace ice when the metal hokey-pokey freezer barrel was removed and in went the coke-brazier.

Carlton Hill corner of Circus Street

The Fishing Industry

The fisherfolk lived in the Upper Bedford Street, Carlton Hill and Russell Street areas. For generations, sons followed fathers in their calling, but their once-thriving industry is now but a shadow of its former self. One or two wooden capstans, the rusting remains of 'chuck' anchors, the great shackles on the Fishmarket Hard, the arches on the Lower Promenade and under Duke's Mound, the pairs of red lights marking the Lift and Fishmarket, still bear witness to bygone days; while now hidden beneath the concrete flat opposite the Lift, beneath their iron covers in the pits, lie the heavy chains to which the Eastenders' larger craft were once made fast. At one time there wasn't so much beach at this point, so during very rough weather the boats were pulled up high, at times across the road and under the Madeira Esplanade.

The names of the fishing marks are still remembered; favoured spots on the sea-bed, rock or sand, in shallow water or deep, the places most suitable for trammel or trawl, for crab or lobster-pot; the most profitable spots to fish, such as Sleeper's, Hospital and Cole's Hole, Jinny Grounds, The Mizzen, Rock Toe, Tar Factory Rocks. Closely connected with the fishing or sea-marks, were the land-marks, many of which are now gone. The pier-heads were used and any large buildings or object breaking the sky-line, such as: Rottingdean Windmill, Hollingdean Dust Destructor Chimney, The Hospitals. At night the shore-lights were used, among them being Old Ben's lights - a triangle of lights on the promenade wall at the bottom of Bedford Street, named after Ben Allen, a well-known fisherman from the area.

By the mid-'thirties the fishing industry was in decline, but the beach still provided an animated scene, particularly during the herring season. Boats would be sailing off, or coming ashore being hauled-up by Stapleton's horse, plodding round and round the capstan, head down, seemingly asleep. On the Hard the auctioneer bargained to the drone of the fish-counters and the hammering of nails in boxes. On the beach, beneath the vats, the fire of old boxes and driftwood smoked as the nets tanned. Nets were spread out on the beach, or mended outside or in the arches, or hung to dry over the railings of the Top Promenade, from Rock Gardens to Paston Place and East Street to the West Pier. There would be much

16

coming and going up and down the gaps, or slopes - those old cuttings that ran from beach to cliff-top, up which the donkeys once carried their panniers of coal, off-loaded from the collier-brigs.

When the bigger boats were putting out to sea they made use of the hauling-off rope, a stout hemp hawser, one end made fast ashore, the other anchored on the sea-bed a considerable distance past the low-water mark. Before the boat entered the water the rope would be picked up and held inboard; when she was clear of the ground, the crew would haul on the rope and pull her out into deeper water, drop the rope overside and make sail. When there was no wind - they would man a pair of large sweeps (oars) rowing out to where they chose to shoot their nets. If there was a steep fall on the beach, the beach or check anchor would be used to slow her down.

In the mid-'thirties a number of the larger, fully-decked boats still survived, some still going to sea, others laid-up ashore, one of them a direct descendant of the Brighton Hog-boat. Inshore, the punts would be under oars in the Roads, the luggers and dandies (ketch-rigged smacks), their galley chimneys asmoke, lay to their drift-nets or towed their trawls, or stood close inshore unloading their catch into the ferries, which plied back and forth between them and the shore. The ferries were heavy, strongly constructed boats, about 16' long.

Throughout the winter, weather permitting, the herring fleet lay off the town and away to the east and west. By day, the stiff black flags of the dans (net buoys) betrayed the presence of the snare hanging below the surface, the long walls of the drift-nets streamed out from the lugger's bows. On cold calm nights, the oil-lamps marking the drift-nets twinkled like sea-stars as they rolled on the swell.

When brought ashore, the fish would be counted and sold by Dutch auction - starting at a high price and coming down. While the counting was taking place, the skipper of the boat whose catch it was would be standing by keeping his own tally. Picking up a handful of pebbles and pulling out the front of his tan frock, as each hundred was called he would drop a stone into his frock pouch. Two men - the tellers, or tallyers - counted, picking up two fish between the fingers of each hand, they threw them into a box or basket, the large baskets being known as prickles. These four fish were together, called a werp, and counted as one. Working alternately, the first threw in his werp and called one, then the other threw in his and called two, up to 20; then one and 20, 2 and 20, etc., up to 30; then two werp were thrown in for good measure, making 128 fish in all - the fisherman's 100. This applied to herring; 132 fish made up a mackerel 100, probably because they were more perishable.

The majority of the local fishermen carried out their business in the waters off the town or along the Sussex coastline. Rye Harbour and Hastings beach were popular ports of call while the men from these places would also put in at Brighton. When the season was favourable, a number of the locals would sail to more distant seas, leaving their home port - Shoreham - sail up-Channel, through the Straits and into the North Sea, as far north as Lowestoft; a long haul under sail and proof of the lugger's sea-going qualities. From Lowestoft they would follow the vast herring shoals southwards, putting in at ports on the way to land and sell their catch. They also sailed to the West Country for mackerel and fished their way back home, they could be away from home for weeks. The larger smacks, also known as dandies, were mostly Brixham trawlers. Ketch, or dandy-rigged, they carried a good spread of canvas, and were faster and stronger sailers than the luggers and more suitable for towing a trawl.

Several factors contributed to the decline and eventual extinction of the local shore-based fishing industry. It had been a living for many over a number of years, but nobody had ever made their fortune as it had always been a game of chance. Nobody knew when they shoved-off from the beach whether they would return with the fish-hold full or as empty as when they set out. Bad weather kept the boats ashore and the market-place empty. When there was plenty of fish and good sea conditions, everybody caught them, so there were gluts and the price fell; herring were sold for as low as 6d a 100 (fisherman's 100) on the Hard and hawked around the streets at 16 - even 24 - a 1/-.

The large numbers engaged in the industry reduced the profits, and there was also the high and rising cost of gear, not the hard-wearing and long-lasting nylon of today, the nets were cotton, the rope was of hemp, short-lived and vulnerable to the tear and chafe of sea-wear, necessitating constant replacement, keeping many forever in debt. During a long run of bad winter weather the fisherfolk were forced to seek Parish Relief - £1 a week, or be offered a ticket for the Workhouse. Given a fine summer, with plenty of calm weather, the boatmen made far more by taking out the trippers than by fishing.

In order to supplement their uncertain income, it was the prerogative of the local fishermen to act as scene-shifters at the Theatre Royal and on the Piers, no doubt because of their knowledge of tackle and hoists.

The fishing families had dwelt in closely-knit communities with much intermarrying. So, when their old localities were demolished, the communities were broken-up and rehoused in new estates far from the beach. For generations, the sons of fishermen had taken up their father's calling as a matter of course. However, as education widened their horizons, providing more opportunities to earn a steady guaranteed wage, they became reluctant to adopt a chancy job so dependent on the weather, with the awkward unsocial hours of tidal work. The large housing and building projects and other public works then under construction offered manual jobs so fishermen often forbade their sons to follow in their footsteps.

The luggers and smacks, manned by locals, were purely sailing craft, and ageing; as they became obsolete, they were sold or broken-up. They were not replaced; and the older men who had known no other life, retired from the sea. They too, were not replaced, so local fishing knowledge and expertise went with them.

When the Second World War came, many of the younger members of the local fishing fraternity joined the Navy, preferring the trawler section engaged in mine-sweeping. In 1940 the beaches were mined and cleared of all large objects, including boats, that would have provided cover for an invasion force on landing. A few large worn-out old boats were burnt or demolished on the spot; many of the punts were taken to Queen's Park and launched on the pond. With the demise of the fishing industry, the beach and seafront lost much of its colour and attraction.

The herring dees were in small back yards such as these

The Herring Dees

Many fisher-folk had their own small dees in their back-yards, where they cured herrings in a primitive fashion. It was the kids' chore to tend the fire, being threatened with dire consequences if it should fail through lack of attention or sawdust. In winter weather the smell from the dees ascended in the still air. There were two large dees in the district, one in Carlton Row being the last in operation, and a mysterious place it was. No small boy ever raised any objection to being dispatched thither to buy two-pennyworth of tie-tails for the family tea, nor did he fret if there was any delay in being served, as this gave him more time to savour his strange surroundings. In the reeking semi-darkness, dimly lit by the eerie glow of the smouldering sawdust heaps, he espied high above him, row upon row of spitted fish, hanging from the long steel rods, pierced and threaded through the gills, while all around and about them there rolled the acrid coils of bitter smoke. Nearby, in the cobwebbed corners of the adjacent out-house could be seen the barrels of brine, containing the freshly-caught fish.

When the herrings were being run onto the rods, the gills would occasionally tear or be damaged, so that they could not be hung from the head; they were then lashed together in pairs around the tails and hung over the rods head downward. These imperfect fish were known as 'headlers', or 'tie-tails', and sold cheaply, as were smoked sprats, tied up in bundles of a dozen and sold for a ha'penny.

19

The Seafront

In the early 'thirties, great changes were taking place on the seafront, many of the old attractions and interesting sights were gone or going, never to be replaced. On a fine summer day - the sea was a hive of activity, dotted all over with beflagged boats, bustling back and forth from the beach. Other 'punts' - local term for any boat up to about 14' long - lay with their bows on the shingle among the paddlers, while the boatmen bawled: "Any more for a jolly ride out?" Pulling a heavy punt with half-a-dozen passengers aboard, all day must have been gruelling work and at 2/- a head - children half price - the money was hard-earned. Although at this time the decline in the fishing industry was becoming apparent, the beaches were crowded with craft of all sizes, the largest being the two sailing Skylarks, clinker-built boats with varnished hulls, yawl-rigged with loose-footed mainsails - to avoid braining the passengers, or knocking small boys overboard with a spar when going about. They seated approximately 50 persons each and operated from the West Street beach.

Completing the vista at sea, were the excursion steamers. The first arrivals after the 1914-18 war were Lady Rowena, Emperor of India and Queen of the South. Operating from both piers, a maximum of three boats came in any one season. One arrived at Easter, the others at Whitsun; all departed at the end of September. It was possible to travel to Bristol by rail and return to Brighton by boat at the beginning of the season. The same trip was possible in reverse in September. These round trips took about three days and the bar was open all the time! On short evening trips music on the violin and harp was provided by Messrs. Alexander and Marcantonio who wore peaked naval-type caps to fit the occasion and collected the cash in a large conch shell.

Before the boating pool and sunken gardens were built, there was a broad tarmac area known as 'The Flat'. This was a popular rendezvous for the youngsters, being excellent for roller-skating, chariot-racing with barrows, and other sports.

Close by the West Pier, well up the beach, the Sand-Artist created his masterpieces, known as sand-scratching. There would always be a lion couchant that looked like the Sphynx, and a wooden-looking soldier - flat on his back, called the Unknown Warrior and a portrait of the reigning King and Queen - complete with Union Jack, all could be viewed from the Pier above, from where the onlookers threw pennies on to a smooth patch of sand, levelled for the purpose. The Sand Artist kept a profitable pitch, his only worry was heavy rain, which played havoc with his handiwork.

Skirting the Shelter Hall - known as the Cow-Shed - at the bottom of West Street, Alec, a small, brisk man was noted for his rhyming couplets. Standing outside his cave-like cafe, he would declaim: "Spuds, veg. and meat. Come in and eat" or "Trays for the beach, one and six each". On a hot day "Come in the shade and have a lemonade". Of an evening, his cafe became a kind of club for the older lads and their girl-friends. Here they would drink Penny Monsters and smoke Crayol fags (3 a penny), flirt, play the diddler machines, and be entertained by the volatile Alec.

At various sites on the beach were the Punch and Judy shows. Sitting on the shingle in a wide semi-circle with faces uplifted, in front of the tall canvas booth, you could hear children's cries and laughter from afar.

After the fish had been sold, boxed and carted away from the Fish Market, and the stone setts hosed down, the Hard became another Speaker's Corner. Here, constantly heckled from the Top Promenade, the political and religious fanatics would preach. More dignified religious meetings would be held here, mostly with a portable harmonium to accompany the hymn-singing. Occasionally, the Salvation Army Band, with Soppy George in the van setting the pace, would march through the town and hold a service of prayer and religious music on the Hard. Here, too, the Happyjackers, driven from their usual haunt by the tide or the law, would sometimes perform.

It was on Good Friday that the old Fish Market became the setting for an annual event and the scene of a lively gathering. On this holy day, when the Bat and Trap Tournament took place on the Level, a skipping festival would be held on the Hard. Two strong men, one at either end, would grasp a 4" hawser or towing warp in both hands and set it swinging over and over, high into the air, loudly thwacking the ground at every turn. Biding their time and neatly judging the swing, then seizing their chance, one by one the skippers would dart in under the heavy rope and leap for their life. Everybody joined in the fun, fat old ladies, beery old boys, giggling girls and high-flying lads, all bobbing up and down in unison. Woebetide any a little late in leaping, the swishing cable had them off their feet in a trice. When a second rope was brought into play, swung at right angles to the first, so that they crossed, only the very nimble could skip this complicated measure. This would be the time for everybody to sing:

"Hot-cross buns, Hot-cross buns, One-a-penny, Two-a-penny, Hot-cross buns all hot".

The East Street groyne at one time had a long seat down either side, on which you could sit and fish, a very pleasant spot on a warm day. The Palace Pier groyne had a lamp-standard at the sea-end. As no trace of the gas-lamp remained, you could shin up the metal post and sit in the cage at the top in the dry, while the spray flew about below.

Between these two groynes, lies the Horse Beach, the bracing waters were said to be beneficial to horses, to strengthen the fetlock's and heal the harness-galls, it was to this beach that they brought them to take the waters. How the horses loved it! They would roll and thrash about in the shallows like puppies, snorting as they made the spray fly. On a warm, calm day, to the delight of the kids, they would join the bathers, with heads held high they would plunge and, like the youngsters, were always reluctant to leave the water. There were a few horse-cabs left on the Seafront, mostly open cabs. During their hey-day there were at least 1,500 registered in the town. At the entrance to the Palace Pier was the stand for the goat-chaise. In their journeyings back and forth along the promenade they would leave neat trails of black and shiny turds known as nannygoat's pep'mints.

During the hot Summer of 1976, the mackerel swarmed inshore, driving the whitebait before them on to the beaches. This was like old times, except that in summers long since past, the waiting boats would have been raced down the beach and frantic attempts made to lay out a seine-net attracting an excited crowd of spectators, who would help to pull it in, with the trapped fish leaping about their feet.

With the mackerel would come the thresher-sharks. When one of these fearsome-looking but harmless dwellers of the deep blundered into the nets it would be brought ashore. In a strategic position on the Lower Promenade, it would be laid-out along the top of a barrow. With its jaws propped open with a stick of driftwood and its long scythe-like tail prominently displayed, it would be exhibited to the public.

A life-saving boat would lie off these popular beaches, the boatmen paddling idly back and forth, ever-ready to come to the rescue. They waged a continuous battle with boys who persisted in hanging on to the sides of his boat, and at low water he would periodically stand up and holler: "Git away from them rocks!", as bathers ventured near the stumps and footings of the Chain Pier that protruded above the sand.

On the Lower Promenade, opposite the Lift, was Jack Shephard's, not so much an entertainment as an institution. This well-known Concert Party performed on this spot for many years, some of the troupers turning up summer after summer and growing old with the show. In bad weather they performed in the Madeira Shelter Hall. At the end of the performance a man carrying a short stick with a canvas bag attached to the end would head for the free-viewers, jingling the bag. Upon his approach the crowd miraculously melted away.

The Lido beach, abutting the Banjo Groyne to the East, was floodlit on Summer nights in the thirties and became very popular for swimming after dark.

HAPPYJACKING

In the summer season, particularly during the August holidays, many of the local boys and girls - with the exception of the older boys who would be helping with the boats - would gather on the beach beside the Palace Pier to go Happyjacking. It was practised mainly by the pupils of Circus Street and John Street schools, who maintained a foreshore closed shop.

There were some independent spirits that gave solo performances, and a boy and girl duo occasionally sang in harmony. Gabbling their peculiar ditties and chants with faces upturned and eyes alert, they would invite the trippers on the pier deck above to "chuck it over, sir! Only one, sir!?" If in response to the appeal for alms, a coin came spinning down, the chanting would abruptly cease, and one of the party below, with hawk-like sight and rapid reflexes would catch it in mid-air. If the coin was missed and struck the pebbles, there would be a dive on to the spot. Much of this activity was for the benefit of the audience; giving them their money's worth.

At low tide they would perform on the sand. Then the coins were often deliberately thrown into the water, into which the boys and girls would scurry a flurry of spray. The victor would surface, and holding the coin aloft, give a shout of triumph. The high water spring tides would force them off the beach, when they would take to the Fishmarket, where they would supplement their musical repertoire by indulging in acrobatics and tumbling.

Very few coins were lost, these being retrieved in due course by the Blacksanders, during rough weather. Happyjacking was frowned upon by the police, whose representative would appear periodically and break up the party. The cry of "Copper!" would go up, rising above the chorus of the beggar's opera, and the tight group would explode in all directions. Some unfortunates were occasionally captured, to be duly fined half-a-crown, with time to pay; this time being spent happyjacking in order to accrue enough to pay the fine.

Another form of reckoning came to the guilty ones upon the return to school after the holidays. The Headmaster would deliver his annual homily: "During the holidays I had occasion to visit the Palace Pier, and saw the following boys singing for money (these words in tones of disgust) on the beach. They are a disgrace to the school. Will they step up on to the platform please." As the dread roll was called, a hush lay upon the gathering until the last name was read, then came a sigh of relief and a lot of nudging and smirking among those who had evaded his eye, though equally guilty.

BLACKSANDING

During heavy weather, when the boats were beach-bound, the fishing fraternity turned their attention to Blacksanding; not to be confused with Beachcombing. When Beachcombing one retrieves whatever the sea has washed up, Blacksanding is the art of searching for, the buried coins and artefacts. The fingers of the wives of many of the habitual Blacksanders were often ornamented by rings of all kinds. This capital could be drawn upon and sold or pawned if the family found themselves in dire straits. Blacksanding is at its best when the weather is at its worst. The sea did the work, sweeping swiftly up the beach, then running back with a dragging action; sieving the rolling pebbles, raking the bottom and turning out the treasure.

Handicraft lesson at Richmond Street school

School Days

Three schools stood in close proximity to one another - Circus Street, Richmond Street and St. John's - all with separate sections for Infants, Boys and Girls. The Circus Street School, still stands. In many cases, members of the same family attended different schools, none of which were very far from home. One remembers the waif-like youngsters from the poorer families, often poorly, yet cleanly clad; and to the pathetic unfortunates from the squalid homes, unwashed and peculiarly pungent, who sat alone in the classroom.

The teachers were firm but fair, tolerating no back-chat, drumming in the three R's by dint of the R's - rote, reckoning and the rod. Serious offences would be punished by teachers with the tawse - a thick, leather strap, split into four of five fingers at one end. This would be administered on the backside or hand in the privacy of the Headmaster's study.

'Nitty Nora' was a sort of small-game hunter, on safari through the local schools. Armed with tweezers and a steel knitting needle she would diligently search the hair and heads of her trembling victims. Should any head-lice or nits be present, she never failed to put on a great show of shock and disgust, which caused secret amusement among the smug ones who had safely undergone the dreaded scrutiny. Considering the cheek-by-jowl existence of the community and the sorry living conditions of some, relatively few cases of infestation were found. Various measures were adopted to keep this menace at bay, regular anointing of the scalp with Oil of Sassafras would decimate the parasites, as would washing the hair and head with Derbac Soap, and by the repeated use of a small-tooth comb, with the head held over a sheet of newspaper. This method was the most interesting, as the crawling beasts would be captured alive, and cracked pleasantly under the thumb-nail.

When inspecting the young heads, the School Nurse also looked for evidence of ringworm, any children found with this contagious disease were made to wear a hat or cap until the trouble was eradicated. Impetigo was another scourge, mostly breaking out on the knees, the virus no doubt entering the many cuts and scratches sustained in the daily rough-and-tumble of school-days.

Upon the return to school after the August holidays, there would be a number of vacant places in the classrooms. When the list of pupils on the register was called before the start of the day's work, the missing one's names would be answered by a chorus of "Hoppin'!". This was the season for entire families to make their annual pilgrimage to the Kent hop-gardens, many going to the same farm year after year. A working vacation, no doubt doubly satisfying to some, for whilst supplementing the family coffers, they were also helping to ensure their future supply of beer. When the bronzed boys duly returned, they were often seen eating enormous apples, as big as their heads - one to a pie - a variety known as Warner King, now practically extinct.

Another answer for an enforced absentee, bawled by his mates would be "No boots!". Although it was the practice with many to go bare-footed during the holidays, this was not permitted at school, however, the Education Authorities would provide the necessary foot-wear. These hob-nail boots, pelted fore and aft, would have suited a deep-sea diver, being quite capable of keeping a 10-stone man on the bottom. To prevent them being pawned, a hole was punched in the uppers for identification. Woollen jerseys were also given to those in need.

The oldest boys would attend woodworking classes at Richmond Street School, under a Mr. Fogarty. At the end of the lesson every rubber eraser and pencil had to be accounted for, which meant the boys grovelling on hands and knees, searching through the sawdust and shavings.

Friday afternoons, weather permitting, the senior class would march to Preston Park to play football, and in the season, to indulge in a little light scrumping on the way home.

School-leaving age at the period being portrayed was 14 years. When aged 13½, I was called one day into the headmaster's study. "Sit down, Robert", he said "Now, I'm afraid that there is no more that we can teach you, so for the next few months until you leave school we'll put you in charge of a class", an onerous task.

There were very few absentees, but should a boy fail to answer the morning roll-call, with no good reason given by the parents, the School-Board would call at his home, to find out where he had got to.

Blood Alleys and Bottleys

There was little money for entertainment, so youngsters organised their own games and pastimes. Many of these street-games were traditional, passed on from generation to generation, and modified in the process. In summer the slower, quieter and less strenuous games were played, while in the winter one dashed about, mainly to keep warm. All these activities were safe to play in the streets because there was little or no traffic. Some of the narrower ways were only negotiable by barrows, being made more hazardous by clothes-lines criss-crossed overhead. An occasional van or lorry would trundle through the wider streets heralded by a cry of: "Look out, here comes a motor!" or a horse pulling a cart would plod slowly past. If a horse and cart was travelling at a brisk pace, it was a common practice to hang on to the tailboard or stand on the back axle and sneak a ride, until some rotter shouted: "Whip behind, guv'nor!", at which the carter would deftly flick his long whip astern, causing the stowaway to drop off.

Among the summer games were 'tabs', and marbles and alleys. 'Tabs' (cigarette cards) were collected in generally fifty to a set - by means of swapping. In the search for cards, all cigarette packets were picked up and scrutinised, and smokers approached and asked: "Any cigarette cards, sir?". The holiday crowds on the Seafront was the best place for 'tabbing'. 'Tabs' was mostly played in two ways: 'drop'ems', or 'flick'ems'. In the former, a card was held flat against a wall and released, the players taking turns. If a card came to rest upon another lying on the pavement, the dropper picked up all those cards lying on the ground. The other method was to prop a number of cards against a wall, and from a line chalked on the pavement, flick cards at them.

The game of alleys was played in the gutter. One player led off with his alley, his opponent tried to hit it with his, each taking turns. When a hit was made, the striker claimed the other's alley, then led off again. An ordinary alley was worth about twenty marbles. All alleys were beautiful, little works of art; the pure red ones, known as blood alleys, were rare. Bouncers (extra large alleys), and the hard-to-come-by bottley too, were highly valued. Some of the earliest types of mineral water bottles, now collector's items, had a double fold in the neck; enclosed in the fold was a glass ball which acted as a valve. Approximately the same size as the normal alley, this was the bottley, and could only be extracted by breaking the bottle.

Whip and top was a solo pastime. There were two types of top - the mushrooms and the peg. The latter took more skill; the former was more prone to fly up in the air and break a window. There were also two kinds of hoop; the wooden one which was knocked along with a stick, and the steel hoop which was propelled by means of a skeeler, a metal hook set in a wooden handle. As the operator ran forward briskly, the skeeler was held low down on the hoop, giving out a pleasant metallic noise. Steel hoops were prone to fracture if they struck the kerb sharply; the blacksmith, who also made them, would mend them cheaply.

The streets were a hive of activity, with all sorts of games going on at the same time: chariot races and chariot fights with barrows, and four-wheeler races and speed trials down the hills were popular pastimes with the fortunate possessors of wheeled carriages.

The girls had their own, more genteel games, such as hopscotch, buttons, skipping, swings. In the game of buttons, a semi-circle was drawn in chalk upon the pavement, with the points touching the wall. Chalk was plentiful - the town is built on it. The semi-circle was split into segments, variably numbered, into which buttons of all shapes, colours and sizes, were flickered, rolled or thrown. If your button fell into a segment, clear of the chalk lines, you won the number of buttons described in the segment.

On the older-type lamp-posts, a metal arm protruded near the top, on which the ladder rested when the mantle was replaced or other repairs carried out. Onto this arm, a deep loop of rope would be knotted to make a swing, with an old coat or cushion to sit on to prevent the rope causing pins-and-needles in the legs. This peaceful pastime had its hazards. On the outward swing out over the road you were liable to frighten passing horses, on the return you risked kicking in the ear anyone walking by on the pavement.

There was the solo performer with her proper skipping-rope, with wooden hand-holds; and the skipping game with a number of participants, played with a longer, heavier rope, with a girl at either end swinging and singing. In a fishing quarter, rope was easy to obtain.

As they skipped they sang: "Salt...Mustard...Vinegar...Pepper". On the last word the rope was turned a high speed, with the breathless skipper, endeavouring to keep pace, bobbing up and down, all hair and legs. Or there would be: "Jam, jam, strawberry jam, Tell me the name of your young man". At which the one who skipped would holler the name of her current boy-friend, and the rope would be rapidly turned to match each letter of the name, as it was chanted.

Many of the street games were played between opposing teams, each having a captain, who was elected or chosen on account of his superior size, the captains picked their teams. If there was an odd number of boys, the two-smallest were counted as one boy.

So sides were picked for what was a glorified rough-and-tumble. The biggest boy in the team would place his palms against a wall, spread his legs for better balance, and bend his back; the next boy would stand behind him, hold his waist or anything handy, and bend his back, and so on, until there were five or six boys in a caterpillar. All being set, the first boy on the other side would take a long run and leap-frog as far forward as he could up the line of bent backs, and there hang on; then the next boy would run and leap, and so on, until the overburdened backs would sway and buckle eventually collapse under the weight.

In the narrow streets, it was possible, with a length of string to tie one end to a door-knocker on one side of the street to another knocker on the opposite side. The culprits would then bang one knocker which banged down when the other door was opened, the string lifted the opposing knocker which banged down when the other door was shut, and so on.

In the barter system carried on among boys, tabs, marbles, alleys and comics were the major forms of currency. These were among the treasures of boyhood, so carefully hidden in secret places. So too, were the rockets for Bonfire Night, the Little Demons and the Jumpers, the Mount Etna and St. Elmo's Fire; so painstakingly collected, bought one at a time over the weeks prior to the great event.

The Catholic Apostolic Church in Carlton Hill

The Church

Ministering to the spiritual needs of the community was St. John's Church (still standing) in Carlton Hill; the Ebenezer (known as the Lemon Squeezer) Baptist Chapel in Richmond Street, since rebuilt, and the Catholic Apostolic Church at the bottom of Carlton Hill, below Sun Street. A little distance up Sussex Street was the Havelock Mission Hall; in Carlton Row was St. Margaret's Mission Institute; around the corner from Sussex Street was the Grand Parade Mission Hall.

The Summer Outing of the Sunday School, generally in June, was either to the Victoria Gardens in Burgess Hill, or to the Orchard Gardens in Hassocks. After assembling outside the Church, and checking tickets to winnow out the usual sprinkling of would-be sneakers-in, the happy and excited band proceeded to the railway station. This being an annual red-letter day in the simple life of the community, a crowd of relatives and friends always gathered to see them off as they left Sussex Street. They waited impatiently at the railway station in an atmosphere charged with excitement, smoke and steam. In the evening, after tea, the stragglers would be rounded up from nearby orchards. Walking down the platform at Brighton Station on arriving home, we would stop and admire the shimmering engine, softly hissing and clicking as the hot metal cooled.

Vice and Violence

The major vice in the neighbourhood was drink. Matrimonial hostility simmered in a few households, when the combatants would emerge into the street - where there was more room to manoeuvre - to settle their differences. The hand that rocked the cradle would sometimes brandish a poker. Between some families a vendetta smouldered over the years, only ceasing when the area was demolished and the warring factions were split apart.

There was an unwritten law to avoid certain streets, but out of boyish bravado, an attempt would sometimes be made to see if you could sneak through unnoticed, this always failed. Someone would spot you and cry: "I spy strangers!", and his mates would pour from their lairs and surround you and your party. As you were outnumbered, it was always best under these circumstances to retreat lest some bully-boy among them decided to punch your head.

'You don't live round here. You're not coming through our street', they would threaten as they hustled you from their territory. So you went to war, with the aid of the bigger and fiercer-looking boys. Passing through neutral territory, interested observers would ask: "You having a war?" "Yes!" "Who with?" "Marine View", "Can we come?" "If you want to". Sneaks would give due warning of your approach, so you would arrive at the gates of your enemy to find him already drawn up in battle order and armed. With a prudent no-man's-land between, you warily stood face-to-face with your enemy; who invited you to step forth and be 'mollysquashed'. Now and again, a braggart would issue from the ranks of the enemy and challenge any of the invaders to a duel. Armed with a broom-handle or copper-stick and shielded with a dustbin-lid, to the cheers of their mates they would thrash and cuff about, mostly in the air, without doing much damage to one another.

If a stalemate developed, or the enemy - although feeling safe and cocky on their home ground - showed signs of weakening, up would go the cry: "Let's charge 'em!". You only charged if you were reasonably sure the enemy would run, but if he stood his ground, he would then charge you, and you would run.

In time, unless the arrival of Tricky Albert prematurely put paid to the proceedings, the din of battle would gradually cease, with both sides under the impression that they had won. Then the enemy would retire and you would depart, with honour satisfied and cock-a-hoop with victory. The jeers, threats, insults, idle boasts and mocking gestures were the munitions of these phoney wars, in which no blood - or very little - was ever shed; a harmless, though noisy, release of youthful high spirits.

All The Fun Of The Fair

All roads leading to the Race course are hills, and up one of these the fair had to be hauled by steam power. The train of heavily-laden wagons and trailers would turn into the bottom of Elm Grove or Bear Road and stop. While a good head of steam was being raised on the traction-engine, the couplings would be checked and the cargo trimmed and made fast. When the safety-valve began to lift it was time to move, and long, slow pull began. With little noise except the fierce hiss of escaping steam and the rumble of the iron-shod wheels; the great old engine surged smoothly and proudly ahead. Last in line rolled the family living quarters and perched on the rear step of the caravan, would be a bunch of swarthy young Romanys, who spent their young lives travelling from racecourse to racecourse; the envy of all the local boys. Towards the crest of the hill, the string of vehicles would turn off the road and onto the grass, and from the traction-engine would come a long blast of triumph.

At one time, the racehorses arrived by train, led from the Station through the street and up to the Race Hill. Highly-strung, sleek coated creatures, in comparison to the ponderous work-horses of the town.

Meetings on the Brighton Race Course were eagerly anticipated and enjoyed by many of the townsfolk, particularly teenagers. In the evening, after the day's work was done, when the punter and the bookmaker had departed from the scene, the lads and lasses would gang up together and hie to the Fair. The dark and lonely hill became a beacon of light and an oasis of excitement. Chair-o-planes, boat-swings, shooting galleries, merry-go-rounds, coconut shies, wheel-'em-in, hoop-la, all the pleasures and the catch-pennies of the fairground were there. The mechanical music of the steam-organs blared forth, mingling with the shrieks and laughter; whilst the traction-engines puffed as they drove the gaudy roundabouts. When the night's sport was over, the crowds stole homewards carrying their hard-won prizes of tawdry china or glass, and shattered coconut, and mourning empty pockets.

The Barber's Shop

The author's father - known as Figaro - ran the barber's shop at No. 11 Sussex Street. Here the hirsute hobbledehoys would come for their quarterly or bi-annual treatment. The charge was 3d. On leaving, they were given ½d refund as a sort of 'fringe benefit' in order to ensure their continued patronage and to encourage the others. Shaving was 2d - no refund. A 1/- was charged to shave a corpse. Payment for services rendered was often in kind - mainly fish, sometimes giblets. On one occasion an avalanche of vegetable marrows rumbled into the doorway as one of the market men settled his score for a haircut and shave. So it became marrow and ginger jam for tea for a few weeks.

Sussex Street in 1932 showing Woburn Place and Nelson Row

At the time of demolition, our parents, four brothers and one sister lived at 11 Sussex Street, the older family members having married and left home. My mother had 11 children; a boy of 4 and a girl of 15 dying of diphtheria.

During the depression of the 'thirties, when there was much unemployment, my older brother and a few friends, fed-up with being idle, all joined the Royal Sussex Regiment.

My father, having his little barber's business to consider, refused to move to the Tarner or Whitehawk Estates, and stayed until something more suitable was suggested; meanwhile, the adjacent properties were demolished. In failing health he eventually moved with his family to a newly-built house in Lavender Street, where he died.

Demolition

When it was decided to demolish the Carlton Hill area, nobody wanted to leave, particularly the older folk, many of whom had spent all their days in the neighbourhood, but one-by-one the families moved away to their new, modern homes, and one-by-one the streets were deserted. Sadness fell on this doomed quarter of the town that for so long had teemed with life. The once-bright little homes became musty, soulless shells; after dark the windows were lightless. The lively laughter and the sound of children at play was no longer heard in these melancholy streets. It was an eerie experience to pass through the dead neighbourhood in the gathering dusk, under the soft glow of the sparse street-lights. The hollow houses, with open doors told of the finality of the departure. The humble homes, within which so many had been born, loved, wept and died, had known so much joy and despair, happy times and sad, now stood condemned and abandoned.

So along came 'Grizzle' Thew - and his dusty men, and knocked it all down; and when the bricks and mortar had been cleared away, and only the footings of the walls remained, it was possible to pace the area where each house had stood, and to marvel at how small a space of ground they had occupied. It was amazing that the warren of streets, courts, rows, alleys, twittens and cat creeps had once occupied so small an area, that so much had happened in so small a space.